D0295280

PREPARING TO LEAVE

PREPARING TO LEAVE

Poems
by

PHOEBE HESKETH

LONDON
ENITHARMON PRESS
1977

First published in 1977 by the
Enitharmon Press 22 Huntingdon Road East Finchley London N2 9DU

SBN 901111 99 6 (hardbound)
SBN 0 905289 00 5 (wrappers)

The Enitharmon Press acknowledges financial assistance
from the Arts Council of Great Britain

Acknowledgements are due to the editors of
The Countryman, English, The Observer, The Poetry Review,
Phoenix, Meridian, Stand, Workshop,
and the B.B.C. Third Programme

Printed and made in Great Britain by
Skelton's Press Wellingborough Northants

CONTENTS

To Aubrey
who left first

BEGINNING

Beginning is
manifold, nameless
pulsing under sand;
breath
expanding folded lungs
in water, land, trees,
blowing blue winds
over mountains, seas;
mouth in dumb moss
speaking wild flowers,
singing leaves into birds,
sucking sinew and horn from heaving swamp,
whirling dust and rain
till footprints name untrodden sand.
Earth, maternal, groans
swinging aside the sea's blanket.
Beginning is
movement
sound
word

THE SIXTH DAY
Talking Beast

On the sixth day
he dispensed with his tail
opened his mouth and spoke.

Words came freely as leaves to a tree
but listeners were rare.
His first love was his voice
too often vanished in air.

So he found a fellow with ears,
never heard what *he* had to say —
words clashed half-way,
unhatched ideas
were dashed on rocks between them.

With her he had more success —
she listened, smiled
then dropped
words like eggs in the soft of his ear.
Out came a weapon to fill the world.
And her voice was stopped.

THE SEVENTH DAY

On the seventh day
weariness overwhelmed Him
before He turned up the sun.
Beasts slept on; no birds sang;
fish froze
in a mammoth grip that made eyelashes icicles.
Mountains, rivers, and holes
were glassed over;
and man's first clumsy kettle
boiled dry at the poles.

Silence
colder than burnt-out stars
deeper than death
ageless as time
till a great laugh
rang through the valleys
splitting mountain sides,
and trees plumed upward in green smoke
fanning with birds
fish twisted in muscular waves;
beasts broke through rocks to lick ~~sat~~ *salt* and rain.
And man rediscovered himself.

RISE AND FALL

I

Summer lies thick along the hedgerows
foaming with chervil
splitting pods and spilling seeds
knees up in the grass, roses in her hair —
fertility act without statistics
or moral, buttons or zips
hindering fulfilment.

Alone for the first time
I walk among Summer's exuberance
shoes pollen-dusted
idly scattering rusty sorrel beads
in concert with the season.
June's hot hand in mine
I swish through plumy meadows to the water
watch moor-hens' bawdy sport among the reeds
where the lake flaps content.
A trout lies shallow, frilling fins and tail;
two butterflies still damp from birth
flicker in heat of a first and last day.
and the warm rise of Summer
sweats under my skin.

II

Why am I sad?
It is Autumn;
leaves fall;
sun reddens early behind the hill.

Somewhere I hear
lifts going down
lights clicking on
and feet hurrying home like leaves.

NASH'S CORNFIELD

These cornsheaves corded waist-high,
prided with the dry bells of harvest,
bow earthwards offering back seed
to the cradling dark,
shadows thrown
silent as barefoot peasants
grown tall with evening,
moving slowly as the sun.

BULL ALONE

Black bull, square and strong,
foursquare against the weather,
steams gently after rain —
bull-vapour spiralling gently into the hawthorn.
But he's young, ready to trample storms;
his meekness breaks under the hedge;
Stretching his neck he bellows the morning out,
trots to the gate barred
against acquiescent heifers,
roars over it his rage and grief,
rubs his sorrow along the top bar
then stands, waiting
like an uncoupled engine, new but redundant.

Alone in a field wide for cavorting
among plentiful grass, unlaboured time,
he is sad as a caged lion,
energy dripping to waste,
triangular, rubbery tongue
mournfully licking his nostrils.

Away up in a gleam of blue
a lark is threading ascending beads of song
above five warm eggs in the grass.
The bull's ears turn, but his senses are raw
with angry suffering smelted in the blood
felt, not understood.

THE HORSES

Between waking and sleep
I am alone in a wide field
drifting towards a closing gate . . .
The gap narrows, and I reach for the latch
but the black stallion arches through
trampling pale hems of dreams.
Nostrils, eyes, sparking the darkness,
rubbed ebony at my thighs
lifting me along where I dare not go.

I left his bridle in daylight;
without reins, I
melt in his muscled stride
across unseen land: no thorn or stone
hindering flight,
no turn for home in this curving ride.
Did we leap the gate
landing free on the far side
with will absolved from need to fight
the dazzling dark?

Time broke with a blackbird singing
sharp as a star
nailing truth home.
It was a journey of splintered hooves
and black miles back to the field
and the white mare waiting at the gate
in first light.

LYRIC EVENING

The afternoon closed round us like a witch
Grey-haired with rain.
In the twist of misshapen thorns we saw her nature
Spiteful and dark
Bent hunchback down to brush the rocky cheek
Of crags in a withered kiss.
The harridan in rusty rags of bracken
Sat in a stone-grey huddle,
Chilled us in scarves of mist.

Then she leapt up and shrieked
Through crevices of deserted cottages —
No moss or fern could gentle that sawmill voice.
And she blocked our road gesticulating
With timber-creaking limbs until we fled
Her raw hill-weather fury.

But as we walked downhill together slowly
The evening rose to meet us like a lyric
With straight smoke from the valley,
And lights pricking their yellow stars
Through winter-roughened larches.

BOY DROWNING

Drowning is pushing through
a barrier like birth
only the elements are exchanged:
air for water.
Then, water for air,
my lungs
folded flat as butterflies' wings
struggled to expand
in a round scream.

Now I make no sound —
or they don't hear
water damming my ear-
drums, nostrils, eyes —
I fight like a salmon on grass
choked with a bubble.
I cannot rise
a third time.

I GIVE DEATH TO A SON

Rhythmic pincer-jaws of pain
clench and widen — the world explodes —
I give death to a son.
Tearing apart the veil he comes
protected fish from dark pool.
I push him over the weir,
land him on dry stones.

Was he anything, anywhere
behind, beyond, out there
in nothingness?
Is he nothing, made aware
of cold, hunger, nakedness?

Trailing glory and slime
he is washed and dried,
graveclothes ready warmed
by the fireside.

BRONWEN

Bronwen with the long brown hair,
nutmeg-brown,
is a strong tower locked from its secret stair.

March hammers the door;
Spring dies hard;
Summer tied by yellowing threads
lies on the floor.

Leaves ghosting up the unknown stair
hurry homeless down,
change to grey from nutmeg-brown.
The strong tower crumbles away.

Bronwen runs to the leafless wood —
no romantic oak for hanging,
no bell-rope there,
only the twist of her long grey hair.

WALKING AWAY

Last night he walked away from himself
along the wet quay leaving his skin behind.
The wind had no teeth for him;
the dark could not blind.

No plunge now in snake-black river shine;
Jesus-feet carry him over
away from sad drunks slumped on benches,
and a woman's whine.

No doors locked; the world swings open
at the 'No Entry' sign.
Through curtains he sees without envy
lovers entangled supple in sleep
and those single figures
stiffening, drying, he fears no longer
since he walked out on himself.

THE CROSS

He was thorn
pierced through my flesh,
twisting away from earth's pull,
planets' rhythm.
In twitching limbs
dance was contorted;
speech leered from his mouth
in frothing idiocy.

Hourly he beat me
with compassion's knobbed stick;
I swallowed resentment
like hairs.
My cupped hands
spilled pity's grit-in-the-eye.

Now he is gone
respite I longed for
sours the tongue.
Silence accuses;
peace whispered through grasses
dies on the wind.
Huge emptiness
engulfs my stand.
He was the cross
I leaned my life upon.

REFLECTIONS

I

The great screw-turner knows
how far to turn
the thread to a hair —
hair-breadth to freedom —
but the thread holds.
One more turn
and I eat air.
Instead I choke
not dead but driven head-deep
into dead wood.

II

I am very small
and must become smaller
crowding myself out
in others' needs
till there is no I
taking up space in the cage.

III

She is untouched
growing flesh like snow
on sapling birch.
But rounding under the cold
Spring has begun
the slow, inevitable
change.
Blood, like snow, will run
urgent, purposeful, quick
under the sun.

IV

He is become sparse
as a larch tree in December
brilliant with frost.
Music of waving green
is sharpened to needles, lost.
Stark, he points to the pole star
north
of fields yellow with sun.
Truth in winter dark
is not to be won through fireside praise
but in lonely pursuit of one hope —
that he may run
blind into what he seeks.

V

Hill creature hunted downhill
trapped between velvet hands.
Under the velvet, bone
hardens in steel-finger bands.
Shrink; the cage presses in.
Only the wind is free —
thin wind, sharp as a pin.
Shrink, shrink, self, away
till searching the hill one day
the wind breathes through a ghost.

VI

The grass's time is over;
many-fingered clover
rusts as we walk the field
no longer loved and lover
but separate to discover
how Summer's juices yield
so dry a harvest.

ONE WHO CLINGS...

I am hollow
sucked at, squeezed by insistent ivy;
suckers have drained the sap
from live wood into gloss —
the ivy is all gloss and green-webbed hands
waving over my farewell,
coiling, clinging
twisting itself into a green tower,
quivering around my life.

'Look,' people say,
'The beautiful ivy —
how it thrives winter and summer
triumphing green
over that broken tree.'

...AND ONE WHO GOES AWAY

Now you are gone
I bleed inwardly
knowing your need of me
matured into a need to be away.

Seasons ahead of you
I am still learning
after growing hard green fruit
in womb and room and garden
to let ripeness go.

OLD CORINTH

The market-place at Old Corinth
has given up its fruits to time.
Roman pavements burn under our feet;
dry flowers rattle like paper as we pass.
We dare not dip into Peirine dripping ferns;
the guide beats us on.
Here St Paul stood in the same sun
that strikes Apollo's temple
making all gods one.

The museum hums with many tongues —
swarming bees around Nero's head.
Escape is the courtyard leaf-and-sun
mosaic under a lemon tree.
History breathes from honeyed stone.

I hardly noticed his coming
so quietly beside me
a pact already made
between two lovers of Greece.
We leaned back into centuries
turning wheels through oleanders, olive-groves,
turning helmets of bronze
where swords sheared the wheat till corn and blood
dropped thick to earth.
Wordless we gathered the harvest alive
shining beyond glass cases and confusion.

MUSEUM

The word *museum*
puts my soul into plaster of paris.
Transfixed by B.C. flints,
moulded to Bronze Age bowls,
my eyes glaze at pottery
fired before earth was round.
I am broken on the wheel —
lapsed Catherine who cannot illuminate
past marvels with present wonder.
History clamps me in iron,
boots me with lead,
and there are stones in my handbag
too heavy to lug around gazing
on monoliths.
In this I am alone.
Around me are rapt crowds
silent as monks,
eyes, lips, mobile with praise;
vested in mystery they pass
velvet-footed from room to room.

Left behind I slip away
through a south door into the sun.
Breathing light and leaves
I revive like a tree
whose frosted armoury loosens in blossom.

YEW TREE GUEST-HOUSE

In guest-house lounges
elderly ladies shrivel away
wearing bright bangles, beads, jumpers
to colour the waiting day
between breakfast and bed.

Grey widows whose beds and meals are made,
husbands tidied with the emptied cupboards,
live in mortgaged time
disguising inconsequence
with shavings of surface talk, letters
to nieces, stitches dropped in the quick-knit jacket,
picked up for makeweight meaning.

Weekdays are patterned by meals —
sole chance for speculation:
will it be cabbage or peas; boiled fish or fried?
Dead Sunday is dedicated to roast beef —
knives and forks are grips upon existence.
This diversion lengthens the journey;
and since Mrs Porter ceased to come downstairs,
ceased altogether,
the ladies at the Yew Tree Guest-House
draw closer to the table.

STILLBORN

Birds pick Death clean.
Death's clean face
is clenched as snowdrops under snow.

And now you're dead
with a snowdrop-face —
too far to go
from darkness into light
when light is not the sun,
sky not the roof
of a sunblind city
birdsong proof
where innocents are strangers.

You were too young to know
yet went your own way
without a step taken
printing the snow.

BRIEF ENCOUNTER

No flowers, please, in plastic hoods —
this will not happen again
and Death's dark angel briefly broods
indifferent to the rain

and briefly opens velvet wings
upon the final scene
to fold them in the nick of time —
the coffin glides between.

A clockwork requiem fades out;
we rise up from our knees
bewildered, and can almost hear
a whispered: *Next one please.*

The 'crem' conveyer-belt slides on
from this world to the next
and everlasting spring and sun
according to the text.

O, fire, is this thy victory —
eternal sun and spring
and truth disguised so tactfully
that Death has lost his sting?

DIFFERENT

Even at school he was different
unblemished by the usual crudities
suffering the form bully without condemning
turning the right cheek
when the art master slashed his left.
The boys, unbuttoning, taunted him:
Blessed are the pure in heart!
And punched him where it hurt.

He walked alone
searching hedgerows for birds' nests;
because he never took the eggs they jeered
hid his cap, inked his face and legs
earning him a thrashing.

Dreaming of a moorland farm
and sheep grey as native boulders,
he was sent to work in the mill.
Under that chimney's dominant finger
he companioned the spinners
sharing their bread and their hunger.
Management exploited the 'peacemaker'
confronting him with angry customers,
snags in the yarn, redundancies —
sacking comrades, they agreed with stroking voices,
was his pigeon or dove.
He was stretched like elastic beyond its give.
Used by all, he was scooped out
till he seemed less than a man,
his cross hollow as a rattle.
So they called an extraordinary private meeting,
thanked him, shook him by the hand
and sent him home with a silver tray.

LATE CHILD

With the children grown and gone
she has another child
born of neglect
of him, their father.
Cocooned in children's demands,
she left him outside her range of love,
remembering to wind him up every 8 a.m.
and shut the door on his life.

He went disregarded,
consoled himself in work and workmates;
football on Saturday;
church Sunday.

Never stooping to his lowered doorway
of high teas, bowls, and workmen's socials,
she left him cold,
consoled herself meanways
in ways beyond his means.

> *Blessed are the meek . . .*
> *Blessed are the poor in spirit . . .*

Already he was in the kingdom.

Now she cannot follow him.
Softly, without reproach, he slipped the latch,
returning, briefly, for bodily needs —
a nannie's services —
and grateful for the little she can give
he touches her hair and hands,
turning the other cheek for her to kiss.

GONE AWAY

When we thought him near
he was away
far side of the hill.
While in thickets we tore him apart,
ate him alive, flung his heart to the dogs,
he eluded us still.

Gone-away fox —
no hounds will bring him back;
melted in distance he runs
through Sirius, Orion.
The hungry pack
trails him in vain; suns
have gone down on his blood.

His breath is autumn mist;
yellowing leaves
glint with his topaz look.
Gone away, away, away —
he is over the brook.

FLOWER

Purple flower, robe of Christ,
from warp of blood and weft of sky,
purple flower that holds the sun
emptied of the cry:
Why hast Thou forsaken Me?
Let me touch your chalice, tip
its juice against my lip.
Save me while I die.

In my rough hands the wine is spilled,
the garment torn; I start
the stony journey self has willed
with soul and God apart.
How may the miles between be filled
now winter grips my heart?

Darkest hour; there is no change
that could not be for light:
star that glitters out of range,
seed defying sight,
besiege the darkness with a power
driving the world's dynamic flower
to open through the night.

THE VINE

All my fruit is yours for you are mine,
The root and stem from which my tendrils twine;
You are the warmth that swells my tender grapes.

My leaves are hands uplifted to your light;
Each palm grows bright to catch the falling sun.
And when the waiting nets of night
Are wide to hold earth's ripeness, we are one —
Root, branch, and leaf and rounding fruit begun
In life's full circle.

White root, go deep
That in your tunnelled darkness I may sleep;
Strong branch, reach high
Till my green hands, glad servers of the sun,
Receive the cup of water and of fire
And find it brimmed with wine —
I drink you, drain you till my life in yours
Is yours in mine.

I CANNOT LOOK INTO THE SUN

In your green anorak
flickering between the trees
I see you, gentle, hob-nailed ghost,
a sack of logs on your back
bending towards the sunset.

In truth, I am the ghost
searching under a pile of summer
for a buried axe.

Everything was lost those last days
when we lost each other —
I tried to hold you back in the dark wood
but a blackbird sang in your head
songs I never understood,
whistling you away from clocks and signposts
up a path I could not follow.

Came Autumn with binding brambles
and blinding leaves
mocking map and compass.
When Winter divided us
I opened the book of rules
and heard Spring laughing at the lych-gate
where shadows change hands with light.

Can you see me wintering in the dark?
I cannot look into the sun.

PREPARING TO LEAVE

Attics cleared; shelves and drawers emptied;
love-letters burned and memory purged,
I knew we had always been
preparing to leave.
Those wedding-groups, snaps of childhood,
babyhood, parents — back, back
to the unremembered, thrust
deep into the dust-bin —
the lid clashes louder than the Bible.

I walk out into wet fields of Spring;
plovers are circling
crying to the rain and the trees,
calling their young from empty nests —
even these
are pulled away on the swirl and heave
of the wind.

THE METHS MEN

A short spit from Strangeways
the Meths Men
huddle together in Nightingale Street.
Rejects among rubble and rosebay
they're doing time
escaping from themselves
drinking day into night into day.

Behind chimneys the moon's cold eye
stares down; they don't look up
except with eyes, shut,
bottle lifted in dummy comfort.

In winter
spit freezes; they shuffle
into the Hostel of the Morning Star.
Last Christmas one chap wouldn't budge
next day couldn't —
hair frozen to ground.
He was only half-dead
so they took him to hospital
and made him half-alive.

Immortality is a long word
and surgical spirit is slow.
Here is no fox's life, red to the death.
In Nightingale Street
dust creeps into mouths and minds.
They die grey.

Close to Strangeways Prison in Nightingale
Street, Manchester, you may see a group of
men, anytime you pass, drinking their lives
away in surgical spirit.

Extract from *The Listener*.

EVERGREEN

Grey from Saxon sky and stone
is this cold day —
church on its cold hill
heron alone
on barebone branch, an elegy
for poets long dead.
Words can tread
truth into the heart
as feet tread leaves
in a woodland path,
truth that grieves
for green tongues singing into the wind
of immortality.
Hope is the only evergreen
that dare not die.